THE WORDS OF JESUS
Thomas Cantelon Publishers

© 1990, R.L. Cantelon

ISBN 0-9626942-1-5

Address all correspondence to:
The Words of Jesus/Missions
P.O. Box 5550
Washington, D.C. 20016

Cover photograph: M.C. Ladenius

"I baptized you with water; but one mightier than I is coming, whose shoes I am not worthy to untie. He will baptize you with the Holy Spirit and with fire."

John the Baptist

"The Spirit of the Lord is upon me because he has anointed me to preach the gospel to the poor; he has sent me to heal the brokenhearted, to preach deliverance to the captives, and the recovering of sight to the blind, and to set at liberty them that are wounded. To preach the acceptable day of the Lord."

Jesus of Nazareth

"For there is one God, and one bridge between ourselves and God, the man Christ Jesus, who gave his life
to win freedom for us all."

from the apostle Paul's first letter to Timothy

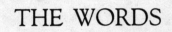

THE WORDS

Part One

THE CHRIST

THE LIGHT THAT HAS
LIGHTED THE WORLD

I have come to be a light to the world, that whoever believes in me should not remain in darkness. I am the light that has lighted the world; they that follow me will never again walk in darkness, but live their lives in the light.[1]

Here lies the supreme test: that such a brilliant light has come into this dark world. Yet the inhabitants of this earth love darkness more than light, because their actions are evil. So it is, those that give their lives to evil hate the light of day, fearful that their actions will be witnessed and condemned; while they that do the truth come freely into the light that their actions may be seen, for their works are pleasing to God.[2]

Once, you went out into the wilderness to see the prophet, John the Baptist. He witnessed to you of the truth. He was a burning and shining light: and you were willing, at least for a while, to rejoice in his light. But I have a greater witness than John; the work that the Father has given me to finish, and which I am doing, testifies that He has sent me.

If I do not do the works of my Father, then you are free to disbelieve. But, if I do his works, even if you don't believe in me, believe at least in the works that I do; that you may know, and believe, that the Father is in me, and I in him.

I must do the work of He that sent me, while it is day: because the night is fast approaching when no one will be able to work.[3]

The lamp of the body is the eye: if your eye be sound, your whole life will be full of light, but if your eye be given to evil, your whole life will be full of darkness; and if what illuminates your life be darkness, how great is that darkness![4]

Aren't there twelve hours of daylight? If you walk by day, you don't stumble because of the light of this world. If, however, you walk by night, you will fall, because there is no light to guide you.[5]

Walk while you have the light, otherwise darkness may come suddenly upon you. They that walk in darkness do not know where they are going. If the blind lead the blind, both will fall into the ditch.[6]

Believe in the light that you may become "children of the light."[7]

You don't light a candle and then cover it with a vase, or place it under a bed; instead, you set it on a candlestick, so that when you or your guests enter your house there is light to see by. Neither do you light a candle and then place it under a basket; instead, you set it on a candlestick to give light to all that are in the house. Don't you realize that you are the light of this world? You are like a city situated on a hill that cannot go unnoticed.[8]

Let your light shine brightly before all people that they may see your good works, and glorify your Father who is in heaven, for that which you do in secret will eventually be revealed, and that which is hidden will one day be broadcast far and wide.[9]

What I seem to be telling you in secret, proclaim publicly, and what you hear whispered by the Spirit, shout from the housetops.[10]

THE REVELATION

The time is come that the Son of man be revealed and glorified.[1]

I do not seek my own greatness; but there is one who seeks to exalt me, and He is the judge of those who reject me.[2]

Your earthly laws declare that the testimony of two witnesses is true. Accordingly, I bear witness of myself, and the Father who has sent me also bears witness of me.[3]

I know that the witness that He has given of me is true. Because of this, I do not require the approval of any earthly authority.[4]

He who speaks only his own ideas, does so to gain honor for himself. But he who works for the glory and honor of the One who has sent him is true, and there is nothing false in him.[5]

I did not come to you on my own, but have been sent by the One who is the Truth. I have come down from heaven, not to do my own will, but the will of the Father who sent me. I was born and came into the world for this purpose: to be a living witness to the truth. Those who love the truth follow me.[6]

I and my Father are one, and in His name I have come to you, that you might have life, and that you might have it more abundantly. I am the door. If anyone enters by this door he will be saved.[7]

All authority is given to me, both in heaven and on earth. I give you eternal life, the keys to the kingdom of heaven, and power over all the powers of the enemy.[8]

So, don't let your heart be troubled or afraid; my peace I give to you, a peace far surpassing that which the world is able to give.[9]

You will know the truth and the truth will set you free; and if the Son of God sets you free, you will be freed indeed.[10]

I tell you this that you might have faith to believe, and be transformed.[11]

This is the will of God who has sent me: that everyone who looks to the Son, and believes in him, have everlasting life; and if you believe in me I will raise you up on the last day. Do you believe in the Son of God? It is he that is speaking to you.[12]

THE LIVING WORD

The Father who sent me has instructed me as to what I should tell you. I know that His words lead to everlasting life; so whatever He tells me to say, I say.[1]

These words that I speak are not my own but come from the Father who has sent me.[2]

They that hear the words that I speak, and believe in Him who has sent me, will have everlasting life; they will not be condemned but pass from death to life.[3]

Listen, the hour is coming, and has already come, when the dead will hear the voice of the Son of God, and whoever hears His voice will live.[4]

Search the scriptures; for in them you think you have eternal life. They testify of me, and yet you hesitate to come to me, that you might receive life.[5]

Though not appearing to you directly, or speaking to you personally, the Father has testified of me. But you are not listening to Him; refusing to believe me, the one sent to you with God's message.[6]

How is it that some of you say, regarding the one whom the Father has set apart as his very own and sent into the world, "He blasphemes because he says, 'He is the Son of God'?"[7]

I tell you now, I am the way, the truth, and the life; no one can know the Father, except by my introduction.[8]

Only the spirit gives life, while the flesh counts for nothing. The words that I speak to you are spirit and life.[9]

If anyone hears these words, and doesn't believe, I do not judge him, for I have not come to judge the world, but to save it. Be warned however; those that reject me and my words are accountable: the truth that I have spoken will stand as their judge on the last day.[10]

Surely the heavens above you, and earth beneath your feet will one day pass away, but the words I speak will never pass away.[11]

THE FATHER

What do you think of Jesus Christ? Whose Son is he?[1]

I have not come on my own behalf, but am sent by the One who is true. Until now you haven't known him as I do, but I have come, sent from Him to you.[2]

No one knows who the Son is, but the Father: and no one can know who the Father is, but the Son, and those to whom the Son will reveal Him.[3]

The One who has sent me is with me, He has not left me alone, for I always do what pleases Him.[4]

He that has seen me has seen the Father; so why do you keep saying, "Show us the Father?" Don't you believe that I am one with my Father, and the Father one with me?[5]

I and my Father are one. Everything that the Father has is mine. I have come from the Father to this world; again, I will leave this world, and return to my Father.[6]

The Son can do nothing on his own, but does only what he sees the Father do. The Father loves the Son, and shows him all that he does; and you will witness even greater works than those you have already seen. For as the Father raises the dead, and gives new life, so the Son gives new life to whomever he will.[7]

That which I am saying to you is what I have said from the beginning. There is so much in your lives that I could condemn; but I have come with another message, given to me by the One who is the Truth. This is the message that I speak to the world.[8]

For God did not send his Son into the world to condemn the world; but that the world through him might be saved. Whoever believes in him is not condemned, but whoever does not believe stands condemned already because he has not believed in the name of God's only Son.[9]

I can of my own self do nothing; as I hear, so I judge; and my judgment is just, because I seek not my own will, but the will of the Father who has sent me. As the Father has the power to give life; so the Son has the gift of life; and has been given the authority to execute judgment, because he is the Messiah, the Son of man.[10]

When you lift up the Son of man (on the cross) then you will know who I am; realizing that I do nothing according to my own authority, but deliver to you that which my Father has instructed me.[11]

THE GOOD SHEPHERD

Fear not, little flock, it is your Father's pleasure to give you the kingdom.[1]

I am the good shepherd. I know those that are mine and they know me, even as the Father knows me and I know the Father. I give my life for the sake of the sheep.[2]

My sheep recognize my voice. I know them each by name, and they follow me. I give them eternal life. They will never be destroyed, nor can anyone tear them out of my hand.[3]

My Father, who gave them to me, is greater than any kingdom or power, and no force is able to pluck even the least of my sheep from his mighty hand.[4]

There are still many sheep who are not in the fold: I must gather them as well. They will rejoice at the sound of my voice, and there will be one fold, and one shepherd.[5]

He that enters in by the front door of the fold is the shepherd of the sheep. To him the doorkeeper opens the door, and the sheep recognize his voice. He calls them each by name and leads them out to green pastures.[6]

When he leads the sheep out to graze he goes before them. They follow him, comforted by the words that he speaks to them. They will not follow a stranger. Frightened by the sound of an unfamiliar voice, they run away in every direction.[7]

I am the good shepherd, willing to give my life for the sheep. The hired-hand is not a true shepherd. He cares not for the sheep as if they were his own, and when he sees the wolf coming he runs, leaving the sheep unprotected. The wolf catches them, and they are scattered.[8]

I am the door to the sheepfold. Those who attempt to enter this fold by any other way are nothing but thieves and robbers.[9]

Such were those that came before me, but the sheep did not recognize or follow them. I am the door. Enter by this door and you will be safe; free to go in and out, and find food.[10]

Thieves come only to steal, kill and destroy: I have come instead, that you might discover life at its richest.[11]

FOOD FOR THE SOUL

It is written, "Man shall not live by bread alone, but by every word that proceeds out from the mouth of God."[1]

I am the bread of life: if you come to me, you will never hunger spiritually again; and if you believe in me, you will never thirst spiritually again.[2]

This is the living bread which has come down from heaven: if anyone eat of this bread, he will live for ever. The bread that I give is my life which I give for the life of the world.[3]

I am the bread of life, and the words that I speak to you are spirit and life.[4]

This then is the bread which comes down from heaven, that you may feast on spiritual food, and, because of this, receive spiritual life and not die.[5]

Don't spend all of your energies for food which perishes; instead, seek after food that will endure forever. This is the food that the Messiah, the Son of man, will give you, for God the Father has given him this power.[6]

You have heard how your ancestors ate manna when they were in the desert, but that was long ago, and now they are dead.[7]

Moses could not give you the true bread from heaven which my Father offers you. For the bread of God is he who has come down from heaven, and gives life to the world.[8]

If you understand the gift of God (and who I am), you would ask that I give you living water as well; for whoever drinks natural water soon thirsts again, but whoever drinks of the water that I give will discover a well that springs up within, giving eternal life.[9]

If you thirst spiritually, then come to me and drink, for they that believe in me, as the scripture has said, "Out of their innermost being will flow rivers of living water."[10]

Part Two

THE NEW KINGDOM

THE KINGDOM OF HEAVEN

Since the time of John the Baptist until now, the kingdom of Heaven has been forcefully advancing, and great is the number that eagerly, and in desperation, have taken hold of its truth![1]

The kingdom of heaven is like the farmer's wheat field, planted with good seed.

One night, while the farmer slept, his enemy came and sowed weeds (darnel) among the wheat, and then fled. When the first blades of wheat finally pushed up through the earth, the weeds appeared as well. Seeing this, the servants of the farmer came, and with distressed voices, said to him, "Sir, didn't we sow good seed in your field? Why then are there so many weeds?"

The farmer answered, "An enemy has done this."

"Do you want us to remove them?" the servants asked.

"No," the farmer replied, "if you pull up the weeds, you will uproot the wheat as well. Let them both grow together until the harvest time; and at the time of the harvest I will tell the reapers, 'Gather first the weeds, and bind them into bundles for burning. Then gather the wheat into my storehouse.' "

He that sowed the good seed is the Son of man. The field is the world. The good seed represents the children of the kingdom, while the weeds represent the children of the wicked one. The enemy that planted the weeds is the devil. The harvest is the end of the world, and the reapers are the angels. Just as the darnel weeds were gathered and burned in the fire, so will it be at the end of this age. The Son of man will send his angels, and they will gather everything that has caused mankind to stumble and those who live lawlessly out of his kingdom, and will cast them into a punishment of fire; a place of weeping and torment.

Then the righteous will shine as bright as the sun in the kingdom of their Father. If you have ears to hear, then listen to these words.[2]

Every kingdom that is divided against itself is doomed; and every city or house divided against itself will eventually fail. Likewise, if Satan is fighting Satan, he is divided against himself. How then can his kingdom last much longer?

If I cast out devils and perform signs and wonders, as an ally of Satan, then what power do your children use when they do the same? Let them be your judges. They can settle that question for you. If, however, I cast out devils by the Spirit of God, then the kingdom of God is come to you.[3]

One cannot take from Satan's kingdom without first binding Satan.[4]

Did you never read in the scriptures, "The stone which the builders have rejected, has become the honored cornerstone; this is the Lord's doing, and marvelous in our eyes?" Whoever stumbles on this stone will be broken by its truth, and on whomever it falls, it will grind to powder.[5]

Behold, the kingdom of God will be taken from you, who listen and do nothing, and be given to a people working to bring forth fruit in their lives.[6]

It is not by repenting, "Lord, Lord," that you will enter into the kingdom of heaven, but by doing the will of my Father who is in heaven.

What would happen if you went to the door of one of your city's prominent houses late at night, after the owner had gone to bed, knocked loudly, and called, "Open the door, I want to come in?"

He would call back, "Go away, I don't know who you are."

If you continued protesting, "But we have eaten at the same banquets and have heard you teach in our streets," he would answer (less politely), "I said I don't know you. Leave me alone."

On the judgment day many will come saying, "Lord, Lord, haven't we prophesied in your name, and in your name cast out devils, and in your name done many wonderful works?"

Then will I have to tell them, "Depart from me, I never knew you. You have lived your whole lives doing evil."[7]

It is given to you to know the mysteries of the kingdom of heaven.[8]

Once there was a rich investor who was preparing to depart for a distant country. Before leaving he called together his three associates, and put them in charge of managing his investments while he was gone. He gave five accounts to one, two lesser accounts to another, and to the third he gave one small account. He gave them each responsibilities according to their talent. Then he left on his trip.

The associate who had been given the five accounts immediately began to buy and sell, and before long had doubled the investments, and had ten accounts. The second associate did the same. He invested the two accounts entrusted to him, and he too was able to double their worth. But the third associate was fearful. He placed the files of his account in a box and buried it in the ground. There he left it for fear that it might be lost or stolen.

Many months later the rich man returned from his trip. Immediately he assembled his associates to give account of their management of his money.

The first associate told how he had invested the five accounts, and now had ten.

At this the rich man said, "You have done very well and been faithful. Because you have been trustworthy with these five accounts, I will put many more important ones under your trust. You may begin today to enjoy these responsibilities."

Then he called the second associate, who said, "You put two accounts into my care, now I have four."

This caused the rich man to repeat what he had told the first associate, "Well done, you have been faithful in managing two minor accounts. I will put you in charge of many. Go to your task with happiness."

Finally, the third associate was called. He said, "I know you are a hard man. You collect profits on other people's money, and I feared that you would only take back whatever profits I would make with my one small account. So I put the money in a box and buried it in the ground, and kept it there until you returned."

To this the rich man answered, "You foolish associate. You know the manner in which I conduct business. At the least you could have put the money in the bank to gain interest. I will take your account and give it to the associate who earned ten."

Then the rich man said to his aides, "Expel this useless associate from the kingdom, to a place of sorrow and regret."

In the kingdom of heaven, the person who uses well what he has, will continue to receive more and more, and have abundance. But those who live unfaithfully, even in the least of matters, will eventually lose that which they have been entrusted with.[9]

Another example is the landowner who went out early one morning to hire workers for his vineyard. Finding skilled laborers, he agreed with them on a wage of one silver coin per day. Then he sent them into his vineyard.

Later that morning, about nine o'clock, he returned to town, and seeing a group of unemployed workmen standing idle in the marketplace, he said to them, "Go work in my vineyard, and I'll pay you a fair wage."

At noon the landowner went back into town, and again at three in the afternoon; each time hiring the unemployed to labor in his vineyard.

Finally, at about five o'clock in the afternoon, he went one last time into the town. There he found a few workers that remained unemployed. He asked them, "Why did you stand here idle all day?"

They responded, "Because no one hired us."

He said, "Go. I still have work for you in my vineyard."

When evening fell, the landowner said to the manager of the vineyard, "Call in the hired hands, and give them their wages, beginning with the last through to the first that I hired today."

Those that were hired at five that afternoon stepped forward, and each received a silver coin. Seeing this, those hired early that morning imagined that they would receive more. When they stepped forward, however, they too received one silver coin each.

Immediately they complained to the landowner, "Those hired late this afternoon barely worked one hour and you have paid them the same wages. We have done most of the work during the hottest hours of the day."

But the landowner answered them, "Friends, I have done you no wrong. Didn't you each agree on a day's wage of one silver coin? So, take what is yours and go your way. I have chosen to pay those hired at the end of the day the same wage as you. Have I not the right to do with my money as I see fit? Are your eyes full of envy because you see me being generous and kind?"

This too is a parable about the kingdom of heaven, for I tell you, the last will be first and the first last. Many are called, but few are elected.[10]

The kingdom of heaven is like a treasure that lay buried in a field. One day a man discovered it. Immediately, he covered it back up, and joyfully sold everything he possessed (considering it a small sacrifice) in order to purchase the field containing the buried treasure.[11]

The kingdom of heaven is like the merchant who spent his life searching for the perfect pearl. When he finally found such a pearl he sold all of his other possessions, and bought it.[12]

The kingdom of heaven is like the farmer who scatters seed over his fields. Though the process always remains a mystery to him, the seeds continue to sprout and grow without needing his help. The soil makes the seeds grow. First the leaf-blade pushes up through the earth, then the wheat-heads appear, and then the grain ripens. Finally the farmer takes up his sickle for the harvest time has come once more.[13]

The kingdom of heaven is like a mustard seed planted in a field. Though it is one of the smallest seeds, it grows into the largest of garden plants, becoming nearly as tall as a tree; a place where the birds can perch and find shelter. It is like the small portion of yeast one uses to make bread. Even when mixed into a great amount of flour, it leavens every part of the dough.[14]

Finally, the kingdom of heaven can be compared to a fisherman's net that is lowered into the water and catches every kind of fish. When it is full, the fishermen drag it up onto the shore. There, they collect the good fish into baskets, discarding the bad. So it will be at the end of the age. The angels will come and separate the wicked from the children of God, casting the wicked into the fire, a place of suffering and regret.[15]

I sent you out to minister without material goods, money, or support to depend on. Did you once suffer lack?[16]

Do not worry about tomorrow, for tomorrow will take care of itself. Truly, there is enough to concern you each day without fretting about the future. Which of you by mental exercise can add one inch to his height?[17]

Look at the birds of the air; they do not fly around worrying! They do not stay up late at night working or agonizing over their future, for your heavenly Father makes sure they are fed. Don't you know that you are cared for as much as the birds?

Are not two tiny sparrows sold for a few pennies? Still, one of them cannot fall to the ground without your heavenly Father knowing it! So stop being afraid. You are of more value than uncounted flocks of sparrows. Even the very hairs of your head are numbered.[18]

Why then do you constantly fret about what you will wear? Look at the lilies growing wild in the field. They grow naturally, without effort. Even King Solomon in all of his pomp and glory was not dressed as beautifully as one of these flowers. If God has so cared for that which grows wild in the field, which is here today and tomorrow is used for kindling, will He not care for you much more? How can you have such little faith?

Therefore, stop worrying, saying, "What will we eat? What will we drink? Will we have enough to clothe ourselves?" (This is the way the unbelievers think, always worrying.) Relax! Your heavenly Father knows that you have need of all these things and more.

Seek first the kingdom of God and His righteousness and all these things will be added to you.[19]

THE ROYAL COMMANDMENT

The most important of all of the commandments is this: Hear, Israel, the Lord our God is one Lord. You will love the Lord your God with all your heart, and with all your soul, and with all your mind, and with all your strength.[1]

And the second is this: You will love your neighbor as you love yourself.[2]

This is my commandment: That you love one another as I have loved you!

There are no commandments greater than these. And greater love can no person have, than he who is willing to give his life for his friends![3]

Whoever lives contrary to even the least of these commandments, will be the least in the kingdom of heaven. But whoever lives by them, and teaches others the joy of following them, will be called great in the kingdom of heaven.[4]

I have told you all of these things, that my joy might remain with you, and your joy be complete.[5]

Surely you have heard the saying, "You will love your neighbor, and hate your enemy."

But I say, love your enemies. Bless them that curse you. Do good to them that hate you. Pray for them that despise and persecute you. By doing this you will be the children of your Father which is in heaven: for He makes the sun to rise on the evil and the good, and sends rain on the just and the unjust.

If you only love those that love you, what good is that? Even the unjust live by these rules. If you are hospitable only to your friends, what reward is there? The most hardened criminal probably does the same.[6]

Instead, love one another as I have loved you. By doing this, everyone will see that you are my disciples, because you are full of such selfless love.[7]

Don't be deceived; if someone truly loves me you will know it. That person will live his life according to my words, and my Father will honor him, and bless him with the presence of His blessing and fellowship.

So, if you listen to what I am saying, and do it, and love me, you will be loved by my Father, and by me. We will come and make our dwelling within you (in the house of your heart).[8]

For my Father loves you, because you have believed me, and believed that I have come from God.[9]

As God has loved me, and I have loved you, continue in that love. Keep my words and you will live in this love; I keep my Father's commandments, and by doing so, abide in His love.[10]

A certain man traveled from Jerusalem to Jericho. On the road he was attacked by thieves who stripped him of his clothes, beat him, and left him half dead.

By chance a priest was walking the same way. But seeing the poor man, he crossed over to the other side of the road.

Next a very religious man happened on the scene of the crime. He looked down on the victim, and then quickly passed by on the other side of the road.

Finally a Samaritan, a man despised because of his race, approached. When he saw the injured man, he immediately felt compassion for him, and tearing his coat into strips, bandaged his wounds, dressing them with oil and wine. He laid him gently over his mule, and brought him to an inn. There he made sure that the battered man was taken care of.

In the morning before he departed, he paid the innkeeper, and said, "Attend to him; and when I come again, I will reimburse you."

Which of these three do you think, was a neighbor to the man who fell among thieves?

Go, live your lives doing the same as the Good Samaritan.[11]

Part Three

THE GREAT LESSONS

THE NEW DOCTRINE

Whoever hears my words, and acts upon them is wise, like the man who built his house on a foundation made of stone.[1]

The rains descended, and the floods rose. Hurricane winds beat against the house, and still it stood: for it was built on solid rock.

But whoever hears my (life giving) words, and rejects them, is like the man who built on a foundation made of sand.

The rains descended, and the floods rose. Hurricane winds blew against the house, and the foundation crumbled. The house came crashing down; and great was its fall.[2]

Two men went into the temple to pray; one a proud, self-righteous man, the other a tax collector (known to be dishonest). The proud man prayed this prayer: "Thank God I am not a sinner like everyone else, especially that cheating tax collector over there. I never cheat, or commit adultery. I fast twice a week, and I give to the temple a tenth of all that I earn."

But the tax collector stood in the back of the temple, and dared not lift his eyes toward heaven as he sorrowfully prayed, "God, please be merciful to me, an unworthy sinner."

I tell you that this man (with such a simple faith) returned to his house forgiven. Those who, in their pride, exalt themselves will be humbled, while those who humble themselves will be honored.

So, let even the little children come to me, and don't hold them back. For the kingdom of God belongs to hearts so trusting; for without a childlike faith you will never enter the kingdom[3]

If any person chooses to do my Father's will, he will easily discover whether my teaching is of God, or whether I am speaking on my own. My doctrine is not mine, but of Him who sent me.[4]

You worship blindly. At least as Jews, we know what we worship, and that the world's salvation is born from among us.

Believe me: the time is coming, and has already come, when people who would worship God won't run here or there, looking for the place where God is supposed to be, saying, "Here it is! This is where we should pray."

True believers will worship God in spirit and reality.[5]

God, the Father, longs for those who offer this kind of sacrifice, of worship and of praise. If you were to hold your peace, then the very stones would shout out.[6]

Perhaps you have read that when King David and his soldiers were hungry, they entered the temple and ate the holy bread reserved for the priests, an act that was forbidden by the religious laws.

If you were a student of the Hebrew laws, you would know that on the Sabbath days the priests that work in the temple desecrate the Sabbath, and still are counted blameless. Now one has come to you that is greater than the temple.

If you knew what this means: "I would rather have mercy than sacrifice," you wouldn't go about condemning the guiltless. For the Son of man is Lord even of the Sabbath day.

If one of you had an animal which fell into a deep pit on the Sabbath, wouldn't you make every effort until it was rescued? Isn't your life more valuable than such an animal?

And if you spend the Sabbath performing ceremonies and observing religious laws; how is it that you criticize me for healing on the Lord's day? You should cease judging by mere appearances, and begin to make right judgments. The Sabbath was made for you. You were not created for the Sabbath.[7]

I have come into this world that the blind might see; and they that boast of their (spiritual) vision might realize their blindness.[8]

THE PROBLEM OF RELIGION

Take heed, beware of living your life on religious "food."[1]

I am not speaking of earthly food. Have you already forgotten the five loaves that fed the five thousand, with twelve baskets left over; or the seven loaves that fed the four thousand, and the plenty that remained? No, I am warning you of feeding on the ideas, and false teachings of the religious.[2]

In vain they worship me, teaching as doctrines what actually are the commandments of men. They're so busy clinging to their own superstitions that they forget the commandments of God.[3]

Beware of false teachers who stand before you in sheep's clothing, but inside are ravenous wolves. They follow their real leader, the devil, and do what he wants. He was a murderer from the beginning, and never told the truth, because there is no truth in him. When he lies, he speaks in character, for he is a liar, and the father of lies.[4]

Woe to you, false religious leaders and teachers, hypocrites! for you bar the doors of the kingdom of heaven, closing the way to those who truly wish to enter: You don't enter yourselves, and you barricade the way to those longing to go in. You steal from poor widows, and then, to cover your real intentions, you make long pious prayers. You will receive great damnation.

Woe to you, teachers and false leaders, hypocrites! for you travel across land and sea to gain one proselyte, and when that person is won, you make him two times more the child of hell than yourselves.

Woe to you, you blind guides, who say, "The temple is unimportant. What is important is the treasury of the temple!"

You fools and blind: what is greater, the gold in the treasury, or the temple that sanctifies the gold?

And you say, "The altar is not important, but the gift that is upon it is important."

You are both foolish and blind. Which is greater, the gift on the altar, or the altar that sanctifies the gift?

Whoever honors the altar, honors it and all things upon it. And whoever honors the temple, honors it and all that dwell within its walls. And they who honor heaven, honor the throne of God, and He who sits upon it.

You tithe even the mint and herbs that grow in front of your house. At the same time you have forgotten the weightier matters of the law: judgment, mercy, and faith; that which you should have been concerned with.

Blind guides, you choke on a gnat and swallow a camel.[6]

You clean the outside of your cups and bowls, while inside they are full of extortion and filthy excess. Blind teachers! First take care of the mess inside those cups and bowls, then the outside will be clean.

You false teachers! In your hypocrisy you are like whitewashed tombs, which appear beautiful on the outside, but inside are full of death and dead men's bones.

You may impress people by your outward show of righteousness, but inside you are full of hypocrisy and sin. How can you believe? You who long for your colleague's praise and never seek the praise that comes from God alone?[7]

You build the tombs of the prophets, and put flowers around the sepulchres of the righteous, And say, "If we had lived in the days of our ancestors, we would never have allowed the innocent blood of the prophets to be shed."

Witness your own inconsistency. You are the children of those that killed the prophets, and now you even surpass the deeds of your ancestors.

You snakes, generation of vipers, how can you escape the damnation of hell? Behold, I will send you prophets, and wise men, and teachers: and some of them you will kill and crucify; and some of them you will beat, and persecute from city to city.[8]

You hypocrites! Isaiah was right when he prophesied of you, saying, "These people approach me with their mouth, and honor me with their lips; but their hearts are far from me. In vain they worship me, teaching as doctrine the commandments of men."[9]

You justify yourselves in front of your congregations; but God knows your hearts: for that which is highly esteemed by man, is repulsive in the sight of God.[10]

I say to you, Many will come from the east and west, and sit down with Abraham, and Isaac, and Jacob, in the kingdom of heaven. But the children of the false kingdoms will be cast out into darkness: a place of tears and bitter regret.[11]

Unless your righteousness exceeds the pseudo righteousness of the so-called religious experts, you will never set foot in the kingdom of heaven.[12]

THE BLESSINGS

Blessed are you who hear the word of God and follow it.[1]

Doing so, you will be like the servant, who, when the master comes, is found doing right.[2]

Blessed are you who put your whole trust in God,
    for yours is the kingdom of heaven.

Blessed are you who know sorrow,
    for you will be given comfort and courage.

Blessed are you who have the humility to recognize your own need,
    for the whole earth will be yours.

Blessed are you who hunger and thirst for righteousness,
    for you will be satisfied and filled.

Blessed are you who are merciful,
    for you will receive mercy in return.

Blessed are you who are pure in heart,
    for you will see God.

Blessed are you who are peacemakers,
    for you will be called the children of God.

Blessed are you who are persecuted for your defense of the right,
    for you will be citizens of the kingdom of God.

Blessed are you when you suffer blame and are spoken evil of for doing my will. Rejoice, and be glad, for great is your reward in heaven. In the same manner they persecuted the great prophets of old.[3]

And how (even more) blessed are you, who having not seen me believe, and keep your faith in me; blessed are your eyes, for they truly see, and your ears, for they truly hear.[4]

Come, you who are so blessed by the Father, inherit the kingdom prepared for you since the foundation of the world.[5]

THE POWER OF PRAYER

Up until now you have asked nothing in my name: ask, and you will receive, and your joy will be full.[1]

Suppose you went to the house of a friend at midnight and said, "Lend me three loaves of bread. I have visitors who have traveled far to see me, and my cupboards are empty."

Your friend might answer, "Please don't bother me now. The door is locked and my children are asleep. I can't get up and help you." I tell you, though he will not get up and give you bread because of your friendship, he will give in to your earnest persisting, and rise to give you as much bread as you need.

Ask and it will be given to you. Seek and you will find. Knock and the door will be opened to you. For everyone who asks receives, those who seek find, and those who knock will have the door opened wide.[2]

In a certain town there was a judge who neither feared God or cared about men. In the same town there lived a widow who continually appealed to him for justice against a person who had harmed her. For a while he ignored her and refused to hear her case. But finally he said to himself, "Though I do not fear God, or care about my fellow men, I will see that this widow gets justice, for she wears me out with her persistent appeals."

Will not God bring justice for His chosen ones who cry out to Him day and night? Do you think He will put them off? I tell you, He will see that they receive justice, and quickly!

And yet, the real question is: When I, the Messiah, return, will I find many on the earth with such faith?[3]

Don't let your prayer fall into a pattern of mere repetition. The heathen pray this way thinking they will be heard by their much speaking. You shouldn't imitate them. Remember, your heavenly Father knows the things that you need even before you ask.[4]

The prophet Isaiah has written, "My house shall be called, by all nations, a house of prayer."[5]

Pray to the Father who hears your most private prayers and rewards them openly; and whatever you ask the Father in my name, He will give to you.[6]

Our Father in heaven.

Holy be Your name.

May Your kingdom come.

May Your will be done,

On earth as it is in heaven.

Give us this day our daily bread.

And forgive our sins,

As we forgive those who sin against us.

Keep us from temptation,

And deliver us from evil.

For Yours is the kingdom,

And the power,

And the glory,

For ever.

Amen.[7]

If you live your life in me, and let my words live in your hearts; ask what you wish, and it will be given to you.[8]

THE POWER OF GIVING

Live your lives, doing towards others as you would have them do to you.[1]

There was a rich man who dressed in purple and fine linen. Extravagance was the rule of his daily life.

And there was a beggar, named Eleazar*, who sat near the gate that led to the rich man's house. He asked only for the crumbs that fell from the rich man's table. The street dogs would come and lick his sores.

Finally one day the beggar died, and was carried by the angels to the arms of Abraham. Some time later the rich man also died, and was buried.

In hell he lifted eyes full of torment, and saw Abraham in the distance, and the beggar Eleazar in his arms.

With all of his strength he cried out, "Abraham, have mercy on me, and send Eleazar the beggar. Have him dip the tip of his finger in water, and cool my tongue, for I am in agony here in these flames."

But Abraham replied, "Remember, my son, in your lifetime you had your good things, and Eleazar such profound suffering. Now he is comforted, while you suffer torment. Besides this, there is a great chasm separating us, so that those who would come to you from this side cannot, neither can you cross over to us from there."

Then the rich man said, "I pray then, that you send Eleazar to my father's house. I have five brothers, and he could warn them, lest they also end up in this hell."

But Abraham said, "They have Moses and the prophets. Let them hear them."

"No," the rich man contested, "if one went to them from the dead, they would surely repent."

Abraham replied, "If they do not listen to Moses and the prophets, they will not be persuaded, even if one should rise from the dead to warn them."[2]

*meaning "God is my help"

There is no generosity in lending to those who can easily repay you. Even scoundrels will lend money when they are sure of being paid back in full. I say, give to that person who comes to you in need, unable to repay you; and if such a person takes advantage of you, don't make an issue of it, or insist on being recompensed.[3]

The poor, when they give, contribute more than all the wealthy donors combined, who give out of their abundance. The poor contribute from their need, and out of love give even what they cannot spare.[4]

But, how nearly impossible it is for those who put their trust in riches to enter the kingdom of God! It is easier for a camel to pass through the eye of a needle, than for a rich man to enter into the kingdom of God. And yet, what is impossible for man is more than possible with God.[5]

Don't store your treasures on earth, where moths and rust corrode, and where thieves break in and steal: But store your treasures in heaven, where neither moths nor rust can deteriorate, and where there are no hazards of thieves or devaluation. Where your treasure is, there will your heart be as well.[6]

Be careful that you don't give your offerings in front of an audience, to be seen by them. This won't be rewarded by your Father who is in heaven. When you bring your offerings, don't sound a trumpet, like the hypocrites do in the temples and the streets, that they may be applauded. Such have their own reward.[7]

But when you bring your offerings, don't let your left hand know what your right hand is doing. This way you give quietly, and in secret, and your heavenly Father who sees such things will reward you openly.[8]

Give, and it will be given back to you in more abundance than you imagine, multiplied, and overflowing. By the same measure that you distribute your generosity, your reward will be measured back to you.[9]

The investment of a rich man returned a great profit. Considering his riches, he thought, "What will I do with my profits?" And he said, "I'll do this: I will pull down my old houses, and build ones that are greater; there I will store my treasures and spend my profits."

"I will say to my soul, 'Soul, you have a fortune that will last many years. Be at ease, eat, drink, and be merry.' "

But God said to him, "You fool. Don't you know that this night your soul will be demanded of you! When you are gone, whose will all these things be?"

So it is with those who lay up treasure for themselves, and are not rich toward God. What does it profit you to gain the whole world, and lose your very soul? What would you give in exchange for your soul?[10]

FAITH THAT
MOVES MOUNTAINS

According to your faith, so you will receive.[1]

Many will come in the last days, from every corner of the earth, and enter into the kingdom of heaven. But the selfrighteous and pious, who continue to lack faith, will not enter in.[2]

If two of you agree on earth, in faith, regarding anything that you ask, your request will be granted by my Father who is in heaven. For wherever two or three are gathered in my name, I am with them.[3]

These signs will follow those who believe: In my name they will cast out devils and speak with new tongues. They may confront serpents, or drink deadly things, yet it will not hurt them. They will lay hands on the sick and they will recover.[4]

Even if your faith is as small as a tiny mustard seed, you can say to the mountains: "Be removed and cast into the sea."

If you believe this is possible, leaving no room for doubt, then what you ask or command will be done. This is why I tell you, whatever it is that you desire, when you pray, believe that you will receive it, and you will.[5]

(As you are led by the Spirit.) The things that you come against on earth will be confronted by heaven's power: and whatever you allow on earth will be that which is according to heaven's divine plan.[6]

Don't be afraid any longer, but believe. Everything is possible to the one who believes.[7]

PATIENCE, MERCY
AND FORGIVENESS

When little is forgiven, little love is returned.[1]

A certain banker was studying the accounts of two people who had borrowed money. One owed five hundred pieces of gold, while the other owed only fifty. Knowing that neither had any way of paying back the debt, the banker compassionately forgave both of their debts.

Which of these two men do you suppose would have been the most grateful? Surely the one who was forgiven the most.[2]

The time came for a certain king to review his records and accounts. During this process, one of his servants was brought before him, owing the king (the incredible amount) of ten thousand gold pieces!*

Since it was impossible for the servant to repay the debt, the king administered the law; the servant and his family would be sold, and their house and possessions auctioned.

But the servant fell down on his knees before the king, and implored him, saying, "My Lord and King, I beg you to have patience with me, and I will repay you all."

The king was moved with compassion. He cancelled the debt and let the servant go free.

That same day the servant encountered a friend who owed him one hundred denarii.** Instead of showing mercy however, he seized his friend by the throat and began shouting, "Pay me back the money that you owe me."

His friend fell down at his feet, and pleaded, "Please be patient with me and I will repay you every last coin."

But the servant wouldn't listen, and had the man thrown into prison until he could repay the debt (according to the law at that time).

Some of the other servants saw what had happened, and being distressed, went and told the king.

The king called the servant before him and said, "You wicked servant. I forgave you your unpayable debt because you asked me to.

*nearly ten million dollars, or 5 million pounds sterling
**a few dollars, or pounds sterling

Shouldn't you have had similar compassion on the friend who owed you such an insignificant amount?"

Angrily, the king turned the servant over to his prison guards to keep him until he paid his debts.

So will my heavenly Father treat you, if you refuse to forgive your brothers and sisters from your hearts.[3]

Don't just be willing to forgive seven times, but seventy times seven times.*[4]

Make peace, even with your enemies. Constant striving will only lead to greater trouble; lawsuits, courtrooms, and perhaps prison, with no way of undoing the penalty except by serving your sentence.[5]

If someone has wronged you, go and discuss it with that person in private. If he listens to you, you will have gained a friend.[6]

Do you remember the saying: An eye for an eye, and a tooth for a tooth: I tell you the opposite. If somebody slaps you on the right cheek, offer him your left, or if someone sues you and takes your coat, then offer him the shirt off your back as well. Someone makes you walk a mile with them? Be willing to walk two.

Give freely to those who ask of you, and don't turn a deaf ear to one asking to borrow.[7]

When you stand in the place of worship, praying, do so with a heart full of forgiveness; even as your Father in heaven offers forgiveness to you.[8]

And should you bring an offering to the place of worship, only to remember an unresolved disagreement between you and another, leave your gift at the altar. Go first and be reconciled with that person, and then return and offer your gift.[9]

Find forgiveness for the wrongs that people have inflicted on you, and your life will be overwhelmed with mercy and grace.[10]

*Don't put a limit on how many times you are willing to forgive those who wrong you.

ON A FRUITFUL LIFE

You will know people by the fruit that grows in their lives.[1]

You are the salt of the earth. But if the salt has lost its taste, how can it be made salt again? It is good for nothing, except to be thrown out and trampled under foot.

Do you pick grapes from thorn bushes, or figs from among briars? Likewise, every good tree produces good fruit, and every rotten tree produces only rotten fruit.

A healthy tree cannot produce unhealthy fruit, neither can a rotten tree produce healthy fruit. Every tree that produces rotten fruit is cut down and used as wood for the fire.

By the fruit of people's lives you will be easily able to see the kind of life they have chosen to live, healthy or dying lives.[2]

A man planted a fig tree in his vineyard. For three years he waited for it to bear fruit, but none came.

At last he said to the chief gardener, "Three years I have come, each year expecting to see fruit on this fig tree, and still there is none. Why should it take up space on my grounds any longer? Cut it down."

But the gardener answered, "Allow one more year, until I've had the chance to dig around it, and nurture it some more. If then it bears fruit, very well; and if not, then you do right in cutting it down."[3]

When your lives bear fruit, my Father is glorified, and you are my true disciples. For a good person produces good from the good that is stored within; while an evil person, out of the evil within, produces an evil (and fruitless) life.[4]

A farmer went into the field to sow. As he sowed, some seeds fell by the roadside, and the birds flocked down and ate them.

Some seeds fell on stony places, where there wasn't much earth. They sprang up quickly in the shallow soil, but lacking roots, were scorched by the sun and withered away. Some of the seeds fell among the thorn bushes, and the thorns grew and choked them.

But some of the seed fell onto good earth, and yielded a good crop; some multiplied by a hundred times, some sixty, and some thirty.

When one hears the word of the kingdom, and fails to understand it, the enemy comes and steals away the seed that was planted in the heart. This is like the seed that fell by the roadside.

The seed that was scattered on stony ground represents those who hear the word, and eagerly accept it, but without roots of inner conviction. The experience endures for a time, but when trouble or persecution arise, resulting from their decision to follow the word of truth, discouragement comes and they fall away.

The seed that was sown among the thorn bushes represents those that hear the word but allow the cares of this world, and the deceitfulness of riches, to overwhelm them. The word is choked, and their lives become unfruitful.

The seed that fell on good earth represents those that hear the word and understand its message. Their lives will yield accordingly an abundant harvest, one hundred, sixty, or thirty times the good that was planted.[5]

HEALTH AND HEALING

FOR BODY AND SOUL

Those that are healthy do not need a doctor, but those that are ill do.[1]

You should understand this, I desire mercy, not sacrifice. For I have not come to call the righteous, but the sinners to repentance.[2]

Shouldn't the sick in body, whom the devil has bound, be set free?[3]

Is it easier to say, "Your sins are forgiven," or, "Rise and be healed?"

That you might know that the Son of man has power on earth to forgive sins, I say to the sick, "Rise Up! Be of good cheer, your sins are forgiven. Go your way, as you have believed, so will it be. Your faith has made you well!"[4]

Who among you, having one hundred sheep, and losing one, wouldn't leave the ninety-nine safely grazing, and go in search of one that was lost. And, when the lost sheep was found, lay it across your shoulders, your heart full of rejoicing. On the way home you would call out to your friends and neighbors, saying, "Rejoice with me. I have found the sheep that was lost."

I tell you this truth: there is more joy in heaven over one who repents, than over ninety-nine persons who need no repentance.[5]

Who among you, having ten pieces of silver, and losing one piece, does not light a candle, and sweep the house, and search diligently until it is found?

When at last you have found it, you call your friends and neighbors together, saying, Rejoice with me; for I have found the piece that was lost.

Likewise, I tell you, there is joy in the presence of the angels of God over even one sinner that repents.[6]

Part Four

THE CALL
TO A NEW LIFE

THE CALL

You have not chosen me, for I have chosen you, and appointed you to go and bring forth good fruit in your lives, fruit that will last.[1]

A man who had two sons told the elder, "Son, go and work today in my vineyard."

"I will not," the son answered, but later he had a change of heart, and went as his father had commanded.

Then the father told the younger son, "You go into the fields as well."

He immediately answered, "I will." (But didn't move one foot to obey.)

Which of these two sons fulfilled his father's command?

Heed this parable: for evil men and prostitutes are entering the kingdom of heaven ahead of you. They have heard the call to repentance and have turned to God. You instead have heard the call and have turned away.[2]

Why do you call me good? There is none good, except God. You know the commandments: Do not commit adultery, Do not kill, Do not steal, Do not bear false witness, Honor your father and your mother. Still you fail in this (by honoring me with your words alone), not using everything, your wealth, your possessions, and your life, to help those in need. Do this and you will have treasures in heaven.[3]

If you wish to follow me, you must put aside your desires, and ways, and daily take up your cross, and follow me. Those who wish to save their life must first lose it: and whoever is willing to lose their life for my sake will find it.[4]

A king organized the wedding of his son, the prince.

He sent his servants out to the provinces of his kingdom to summon those that were invited to the wedding, but the guests refused to come.

So the king sent out his servants, saying, "Tell those invited to the wedding, I have prepared a great dinner. My oxen and best calves have been killed, and everything is ready. Come to the wedding."

But the subjects made light of this invitation as well, and turned away; some to their farms, others to their businesses in town. The subjects who remained then seized the king's servants and beat them to death.

When the king learned of what had been done he was enraged. Immediately he sent out his palace soldiers. They gathered the murderers, executed them, and burned their houses to the ground.

Then he said to his servants, "The wedding is ready, but those that were invited were not worthy to attend. Go then, to those that you meet on the street corners and on the road outside the city, and invite them to the wedding celebration."

So the king's servants went to the street corners of the city, and then out along the highways, and invited everyone they encountered, both the good and the bad, and the wedding hall was filled with these guests.

But when the king came in to see his guests, he was shocked to see one eating without the wedding garment (that had been provided). He asked, "How is it that you came in to the feast without your wedding garment?"

But the man gave no answer.

Then the king said to his servants, "Bind this man hand and foot, take him away, and cast him out into the darkness, where there are tears of regret and sorrow."

For I tell you, many are called (into the kingdom) but few are chosen.[5]

The time has come. The kingdom of God is at hand. I have chosen you out from the world's way of living life. Repent, and believe the gospel.[6]

No one can come to me unless the Father, who has sent me, draws him; and I will raise up that person on the last day. All of you whom the Father has given me will come to me: and whoever comes to me, I will never, ever refuse.[7]

Because I have told you such things, do you believe? Truly, you will see even greater things than these.[8]

Enter therefore through the narrow gate, for wide is the path, and broad is the way, that leads to destruction, and many go through that gate: but narrow is the gate and the way, which lead to life, and there are few that find it. So make every effort to go through the gate that leads to life. One day, many will suddenly want to change their way for the right way, and it will be too late.[9]

ON BEING BORN AGAIN

Don't be amazed that I say you must be born again.[1]

Truly I tell you, unless you are born again, you cannot see the kingdom of God. Except you are born of water and the Holy Spirit, you cannot enter the kingdom of God.[2]

That which is born of flesh is flesh; and that which is born of Spirit is spirit. The wind blows where it wishes, and we hear the sound it makes, but we cannot tell from where it comes, or where it will go. So it is for everyone that is born of the Spirit.[3]

No one weaves a piece of new cloth into an old rotting garment, for the new which is woven in will just pull the old cloth apart, and the tear will be made worse. Neither do you put new wine into old wine barrels. You would fear that the old barrels would break, the new wine run out, and the investment be lost. Instead, you put new wine into new barrels, and both are preserved.[4]

How is it that with so much learning you still aren't aware of these truths? If I have told you such things, using earthly examples, and you don't understand, how will you understand if I tell you of heavenly things?[5]

For God sent not his Son into the world to condemn the world; but that the world through him might be saved. Whoever believes in him is not condemned, but whoever does not believe stands condemned already because they have not believed in the name of God's only Son.[6]

I am the resurrection and the life. Whoever believes in me, though they die on this earth, will live again. They will be given eternal life and not perish! I have told you so many times, If you believe you will see the glory of God.[7]

My mission is to accomplish the purpose of Him that sent me, and to fulfill his work; and this is God's will: That you come to truly believe in him, the Messiah, whom He has sent.[8]

A man had two sons. One day the younger son said to his father, "Father, give me my part of the inheritance." So the father gave him his share.

Not long afterwards the younger son gathered his possessions, and journeyed to a far country. There he wasted his wealth in reckless living.

When his last penny was gone, a terrible famine swept across the land. His situation grew continuously worse.

Finally he found employment, working for a citizen of that country, tending pigs.*

In his desperation, he was about to eat the corn husks that he fed the pigs, when coming to his senses he thought, "My father's many servants have more than enough bread to eat, with much left over, while I am about to eat pigs' food in order not to perish with hunger! I will return to my father, and will say, 'Father, I have sinned against you and heaven. I am no longer worthy to be called your son. Let me be at least one of your hired servants.' "

With this plan in mind, he rose from the dust and began the long trip back to his father.

When he was still a great way off, his father saw him, and having compassion on him, ran, and threw his arms around him in a tender embrace.

The son began, "Father, I have sinned against heaven and in your sight, and am no longer worthy to be called your son."

But the father said to his servants, "Bring out my best suit, and dress my son. Put my signet ring on his hand, and my best shoes on his feet. Bring our fattest calf from the field, and kill it, and let us eat, and be merry. For this my son was dead, and is alive again; he was lost, and now is found." Then began a great celebration.

About this time his older brother returned from working in the field, and as he came near the house he heard the music and dancing. He called one of the servants, and asked, "What is the meaning of such celebration?"

The servant replied, "Your younger brother has come home, and your father has killed the fattest calf, because he has returned safe and sound."

*a practice that violated his religious upbringing

At this the brother became very angry, and refused to go in to the banquet, so that his father came out, and begged him to come in.

But he answewred, "Behold all these years I have served you, never breaking one of your commandments, yet you never offered me parties to celebrate with my friends. Now my wandering brother returns, who has, no doubt, wasted his inheritance on prostitutes, and you kill the best calf to celebrate."

The father said, "My son, you have always been with me, and you know that all that I have is yours. It is right that we celebrate, and give thanks, for your brother was dead, and is alive again; was lost, but now is found."[9]

Except you be converted, and become as a little child, you will not enter the kingdom of heaven. The Son of man is come to save those that are lost; for it is not the will of your Father which is in heaven, that even the least among you should perish.[10]

For God so loved the world, that He gave his only Son, that whosoever believes in him should not die, but have everlasting life. Do you believe this?[11]

DISCIPLES AND SERVANTS

You cannot allow two masters to rule your life. You will either hate one, and love the other, or else cling to one, and despise the other. You cannot serve God and remain a slave to the gods of this world.[1]

Which one of you, planning to build a tower, wouldn't first sit down and estimate the cost, making sure there was enough money to finish it? Otherwise, you may lay the foundation, and then be forced to abandon the project. Those who had been observing your progress would laugh at you, and say, "He began to build, but now he is bankrupt."

Can you imagine a great king preparing to defend his kingdom against an invading army, without first sitting down with his military advisors to consider whether his army of ten thousand would be able to defeat the enemy's force of twenty thousand? If his advisors see no chance of victory, the king will quickly send his ambassadors to meet the approaching enemy, and attempt to negotiate peace before the battle begins.

Unless you are willing to count the cost, and make a total commitment, you cannot truly follow me.[2]

One day a very rich man was informed that his trusted accountant was stealing from his investments. He called the man, and asked, "Why do I hear these accusations against you? Show me the records, or you will no longer be trusted with my accounts."

Then the accountant reasoned to himself, "What will I do? If he examines the books, I'll be sent away. I'm two weak to do manual labor, and too proud to beg."

He devised a cunning plan so that, should he be fired, he would be in good favor with his master's debtors, and welcome among them. First he summoned each person that was in debt to his master, and asked, "How much do you owe?"

The first answered, "One hundred gallons of oil."

"Here," said the accountant, "take your bill and write down fifty."

To the next in line he asked again, "How much do you owe?"

"One thousand bushels of wheat," was the reply.

The accountant said, "Take your bill and write down eight hundred."

When the employer learned what his scheming accountant had done, instead of being angry, he only commended him for his shrewdness.

How is it that the children of this world, in this generation, though they act dishonestly, are often more clever than the children of the truth? But should you live by such rules, buying friendship through cheating? Will this way of living ensure your entry into an everlasting heavenly home? No, let me remind you; the person who is diligent in small things, will also be trusted with much, and the person who is dishonest with little things will also be dishonest with much. If you can't be trusted with earthly riches, how can you be trusted with true spiritual riches? And if you haven't been faithful with what belongs to another, who will offer you riches of your own?[3]

I send you out as sheep among wolves: so be as wise as serpents, but harmless as doves.[4]

You have seen how the kings and great rulers of the earth exercise their authority, and lord it over the poor people beneath them. This is not true for you who belong to the kingdom of God. Whoever would be great among you, must first be your servant. And whoever of you would be the greatest, must first be servant of all.[5]

Even so I, the Messiah, came not to be served, but to serve, and to give my life as a ransom for many.[6]

If you know these things, happy are you if you do them.[7]

Continue in the light of my word; then you are truly my disciples.[8]

Don't be like the falsely religious, inventing laws and ordinances. They glory in their rules, and then don't follow even one of them. They lay burdens of legalism on the necks of their followers, while they wouldn't dream of observing such rules.

They go to great lengths to be seen by you, wearing exaggerated garments, behaving with great ceremony, seated at the head tables and on the front row. They love to be called "esteemed" and "learned teacher." But you shouldn't be called "esteemed" or "master," for you have only one master and you are all his brothers and sisters. Refrain from calling them "father," for you have one Father in heaven. Neither allow anyone to call you "learned teacher," for there is one teacher, Christ.

The one who is greatest among you must first be your servant. Those who imagine themselves to be great will be humbled; and those who humble themselves will be exalted.[9]

When the Messiah returns in his glory, and all the holy angels with him, he will sit on the throne of his heavenly glory. Before him will be gathered all nations; and he will separate the people one from another, as a shepherd divides the sheep from the goats. The sheep he will set on his right hand, and the goats on his left.

Then the King will say to those on his right hand, "Come, blessed by my Father; enter into the inheritance of the kingdom, prepared for you since the foundation of the world. For I was hungry, and you offered me food. I was thirsty, and you brought me something to drink. I was a stranger, and you invited me in. I was without clothes, and you clothed me. I was ill, and you cared for me. I was in prison, and you visited me."

Then the rightous will answer in amazement, "Lord, when did we see you hungry, and feed you, or thirsty, and give you something to drink? When did we see you as a stranger, and give you shelter, or needing clothes, and clothe you? Did we ever see you ill, and take care of you, or in prison and visit you?"

The King will reply, "Truly, I tell you now; inasmuch as you have done these things for the least of my brothers and sisters, you have done the same for me."

But to the ones on his left, the King will say: "Depart from me. For I was hungry, and you gave me no food. I was thirsty, and you offered me nothing to drink. I was a stranger, and you turned me away. I was naked, and you gave me no clothes. I was sick, yet you didn't care for me. I was in prison, but you didn't visit me."

Then they will answer him, "Lord, when did we see you hungry, or thirsty, or a stranger, or naked, or sick, or in prison, and did not comfort you?"

The King will answer, "Truly I say to you; inasmuch as you have failed to do these things for the least of my brothers and sisters, you have failed to do them for me."

These then will be sent away into everlasting punishment, but the righteous to life eternal.[10]

You call me Master and Lord, and you are correct, for so I am. If I then, your Lord and Master, am willing to be your lowest servant, then you too should be willing to serve one another. I have given you an example; you should do the same as I have done for you.[11]

THE GREAT COMMISSION

As the Father has sent me, so I am sending you.[1]

Let those who are spiritually dead attend to their earthly concerns; but you go and proclaim the coming of the kingdom of God to the (waiting) world.[2]

There is a great harvest before you, but sadly, the laborers are few: pray to the Lord of the harvest, that He will send more laborers to collect his harvest. No one who puts his hand to the plow and then looking back, longs to abandon the mission, is suitable for the kingdom of God.[3]

You who believe in me will do the same works that I do, and greater (for I must return to my Father in Heaven).[4]

If you wish to serve me, follow me; and where I am, there you, my servant, will be as well, and honored by my Father.[5]

Go, announce, "The kingdom of heaven has come to you."

Heal the sick, restore the lepers to health, raise the dead, cast out devils! Remember what I have told you, "Freely you have received this new life. Freely give!"[6]

Those trying to save their lives will, in the end, lose them; but those willing to lose their lives for my sake, will discover life. If you are not for me, you are against me; and they that do not gather with me scatter.[7]

Whenever you are invited into a house, offer a blessing, and say, "Peace be to this house." If those in the house be for peace, your blessing will be accepted, and they will be benefitted. If not, the benefits of your blessing will return to you.

Don't hesitate to accept hospitality (yet remain purposeful, and resist wandering about aimlessly). Enjoy whatever food and drink is offered you, for a working person is worthy of his wages.[8]

They that will receive the person I send out with this message, also receive me, and they that receive me, receive He who sent me.[9]

Be warned, there are some who would attempt to silence your voices; who would take you to court, and deal unfairly with you, even seeking your imprisonment. Because of my message you will be called to testify before those who do not believe; rulers, governors, and kings.[10]

If you are accused and brought to court, don't fear for your lack of words. They will be given to you in that instant. You need not rely on your words alone, for the Spirit of your Father will speak through you.

Remember (in the earthly kingdom) no servant is greater than his master. If they have persecuted me, they will also persecute you; punishing you for my cause (not realizing who it was that sent me into the world). If, however, they accept and follow my message, they will accept and follow yours as well.[11]

If I had not come with the message of truth, the inhabitants of the world would not have been aware of their failings and sinful behavior. Now they have no way of hiding their deeds (behind their former ignorance of the truth). If I had not performed such mighty miracles among them, they would not have realized their shortcomings. But now (those who have rejected the truth) have seen the miracles, and hated me and my Father.[12]

This is come to pass, that the prophecy might be fulfilled, "They hated me without a cause."[13]

It is a fire that I have come to bring upon the earth. How I long to see it ablaze! Did you imagine that I had come to bring calm and tranquility to earth? No, I tell you, I have come to bring division: For from now on there will be five in one house, divided on what they should believe, three against two, and two against three.

A father will be divided against his son, and the son against his father; the mother against her daughter, and the daughter against her mother; the mother-in-law against her daughter-in-law, and the daughter-in-law against her mother-in-law. Brothers will betray their brothers to death, and fathers their children. Children will rise up against their parents, and cause them to be put to death.[14]

When you are comforted by the world's hatred, remember how it hated me before.[15]

And, if they persecute you in one place, move on to the next. You will not have reached all the cities of the world before the Messiah returns. If a city refuses to accept you, or listen to your message, shake the dust of that city from your feet as you leave. Believe me, in the day of the final judgment, it will have been better to be from the land of Sodom and Gomorrah than from that city.[16]

If you followed the world's way of doing things, the world would love you. But because you follow the ways of the kingdom, as I have called you into the kingdom, the world despises and hates you.[17]

Whoever hears the words that you speak hears me, and those that despise you (because of your true words) despise me. In rejecting me, they reject Him who sent me.[18]

Endure the criticism of skeptics and doubters for my name's sake. Stand firm, in so doing you will be saved.[19]

These worcs I have spoken to you, that in me, and in following my words, you might find peace. In the world you will have pain and trouble, but be happy, for I have overcome the world.[20]

Therefore, go throughout the world and preach the gospel. For the Son of Man has not come to destroy lives, but to save them.[21]

CHRIST'S PRAYER
FOR HIS DISCIPLES

Father, the hour is come. Glorify your Son so that he can bring glory to you, for you have given him authority over every man and woman on earth, that he might give eternal life to those you have given him.[1]

And this is life eternal: That they might know you, the only true God, and Jesus Christ, whom you have sent.

I have glorified you on earth by completing the work that you gave me to do. Now, Father, reveal my glory as I stand in your presence, the glory I had with you since before the world began. I have revealed you to those that you gave me out of the world. They were yours, and you gave them to me, and they have accepted your word. Now they know that everything you have given me comes from you. I have faithfully delivered to them the words that you gave me, they have believed them, and have come to know in their hearts that I have come from God, sent by you to them.

I am not praying for the world, but for those you have given me, for they truly are yours. All of these, who have believed in me, are yours, and they do honor me. I am returning to you in heaven, but those that believe in me remain in this world. Father, keep them by the power of your name; that they all may be one, as we are one.

While I was with them in the world, I kept them by the power that you gave me; I guarded them and not one was lost (except for the son of destruction, that the scripture might be fulfilled)* Now I am coming to you, but I say these things while I am in the world, that they might experience the full measure of joy in their hearts.

I have given them your word, and the world has hated them, because they are no longer children of this (dark and dying) world, even as I am not. I am not asking that you take them out of the world, but that you keep them safe from the evil one, for they are no more children of darkness than I am. Make them holy by your truth, for your word is truth.

As you have sent me into the world, so I send them into the world. And for their sakes I consecrate myself that they may be made holy, and grow in truth.

I do not pray for these only, but also for the future believers who will come to believe in me because of the testimony that they

*meaning Judas

give. Let them all be of one heart and mind, just as you and I are one; that as you are in me, and I in you, they will be in us, and the world will know that you sent me.

I have given them the glory that you gave me; that they may be one, even as we are one: I in them, and you in me, being perfected into one, that by this the world will fully understand that you have sent me, and have loved them as much as you have loved me. May they (one day) be with me where I am; beholding my glory, which you have lovingly given me since the foundation of the world.

Father of goodness and truth, the world has not known you, but I have known you, and these who believe in me know now that it is you who sent me.

I have made you known to them, and will continue to reveal you to them, that the love you have for me may dwell in their hearts, and that I may dwell there as well. So be it.[2]

Part Five

THE LAST DAYS
OF CHRIST ON EARTH

THE BETRAYAL

How is it you betray the Son of man with a kiss, arresting me
as if I were a thief, carrying swords and clubs? Daily I was among
you in the temple, and you never laid a hand on me. But this
is your hour and the power of darkness is at work.[1]

All things that were written by the prophets concerning the Messiah will be fulfilled. He will be delivered into the custody of the heathen, mocked, treated spitefully, and misused. They will beat him, and put him to death, but on the third day he will rise again.[2]

Soon I must leave this earth and go, where as yet you cannot follow. I have longed to eat this passover with you before I suffer; for I tell you in truth: I will not eat the passover again, until all that it signifies be fulfilled in the kingdom of God, nor will I drink of the fruit of the vine, until the kingdom of God has come. This bread is my body which is given for you. Eat it in remembrance of me. This wine represents God's new covenant of salvation, sealed by my blood, which I pour out on your behalf.[3]

I must give my life, as was foretold by the prophets, but woe to the man who betrays the Son of man. It would have been better if that man had not been born. I am not saying this of all of you, for I know very well those whom I have chosen, but the scripture must be fulfilled which says, "One who shares my bread will betray me."[4]

I tell you this now, before it comes to pass, that afterwards, you will believe in me.[5]

Do you boast that you are willing to lay down your life for my sake? Sadly, you will all desert me on this night, as the prophets have written, "I will strike the shepherd, and the sheep will be scattered."[6]

O, Father, if it be possible, let this ordeal pass from me. Nevertheless not my will, but your will be done.[7]

Behold, the hour has come for the Son of man to be betrayed into the hands of sinners.[8]

Beware, those who live by the sword will die by the sword.[9]

Don't you realize that I could pray to my father, and He could send down twelve legions of angels for my defense? But, how then could the scriptures be fulfilled that say it must happen this way?[10]

Now the Son of man will be glorified, and God will be glorified in him.[11]

THE TRIAL

You can have no power at all against me, unless it is given to you from above.[1]

Why do you try me by asking these questions? You should ask those who have listened to me instead. They know very well the things I have said.

I have not whispered my message in secret. I have spoken openly to the world. I have taught in the places of worship and publicly in the temple, where my followers gathered.

If what I have said is wrong, then give evidence of this. But if I have spoken the truth, then why do you strike me?[2]

My kingdom is not of this world. If my kingdom were of this world my followers would have taken up arms to defend it, that I should not be delivered into your hands. But my kingdom is not of this earth.

Yet, you are right when you accuse me of being a king. To this end was I born, and for this purpose I came into the world, that I should be a witness to the truth.

All who love the truth recognize my message.[3]

THE CROSS

Now will the prince of this world be overthrown, and if I be
lifted up from the earth (on the cross) I will draw all people to me.[1]

Because of this my Father loves me, for I lay down my life, that I might take it back again. No man takes it from me, but I lay it down of my own free will. I have the power to lay it down and I have the power to take it again. The Father has given me this power and right.[2]

Father, forgive them; for they know not what they do.[3]

Truly I say to you, today you will be with me in paradise.[4]*

Woman, behold your son![5]**

Behold your mother![6]***

Eloi, Eloi, lama sabachthani?[7]****

I thirst.[8]

It is finished.[9]

Father, into your hands I commit my spirit.[10]

*To the thief on the cross.[4]

**To Mary standing at the foot of the cross with John.[5]

***To John.[6]

****My God, my God, why have you forsaken me?[7]

FOLLOWING
THE RESURRECTION

Don't be faithless any longer, but believe.[1]

I know where I have come from, and where I will go; but you cannot tell where I have come from, or where I am going. You are from the earth. I am from above. You are of this world. I am not of this world.[2]

No one has ascended up to heaven, except he that came down from heaven, the Son of God who is in heaven.[3]

Go tell my brothers that I will ascend to my Father, and your Father; and to my God, and your God.[4]

Why are you troubled, and doubts arise in your minds? Be in peace.[5]

Behold my hands and my feet, that it is I myself: touch me, and see; for a spirit doesn't have flesh and bones, as you see I have.[6]

Because you have seen me, you believe. Blessed are you that have not seen me and believe.[7]

In a little while, the world will see me no more; but my presence will remain with you; and because I live, you will live also.[8]

Part Six

THE PROMISE

THIS GENERATION

Whoever is ashamed of me and of my words in these days of sin and unbelief; of that person will the Son of man be ashamed when he returns in the glory of His Father and the holy angels.[1]

Still unbelieving, this apostate generation clamors for a sign, and no sign will be given than the sign of the prophet Jonah. For, just as Jonah was in the great whale for three days and nights, so the Son of man will be buried three days and nights in the earth.

Truly, there will come a day when the inhabitants of Nineveh (the capital city of Assyria, known as the "City of Thieves") will stand in judgment of this generation, and condemn it; for they repented because of the preaching of Jonah, and now a greater than Jonah stands before you. The Queen of Sheba will also rise in judgment of this generation, and condemn it; for she traveled a great distance to hear the wisdom of Solomon, and behold, a greater wisdom than Solomon has come.[2]

How can I describe this generation? They are like children sitting in the market place, calling to their friends, "We played on our flutes, but you wouldn't dance, or sing. So we played a dirge, but you refused to be sad."

John, the forerunner, came and lived among you in austerity. Everyone said, "He must have a demon." Now, the son of man has come to you enjoying life to its full, and you say, "A drunkard and a glutton, the friend of low-lifes and sinners!" With such brilliance, you justify your own inconsistencies![3]

Oh generation, who live your lives based on lies, how can you, being evil, speak any good thing? For, out of the abundance of the heart the mouth speaks.[4]

When it is evening, you say, "It will be fair weather for the sky is red." And in the morning you say, "It will be foul weather today, for the sky is red and threatening." You can accurately forecast the weather. Can't you discern the signs of the times?[5]

Come to me, all of you, tired, oppressed, and sick of life, and I will give you wonderful rest! Take my yoke upon you, learn what I am saying; I am gentle and have a humble heart. At last you will find rest for your souls, for my heaviest burden is light.[6]

Truly, those of you who have chosen to follow me in this generation, will one day sit upon thrones and judge the kingdoms, and those who have turned away from these righteous words.[7]

ALL THINGS

Oh fools, and slow to believe all that the prophets have spoken. Shouldn't Christ have suffered all of these things and then enter into his glory?[1]

This is what I was telling you, when I was among you, that all things must be fulfilled, which were written in the law of Moses, the prophets and the Psalms, concerning me: that Christ had to suffer, and rise from the dead on the third day, and that repentance and forgiveness of sins would be preached in his name among all nations, beginning at Jerusalem.[2]

I tell you, that many prophets and kings have desired to see the things that you see, and have not seen them, and to hear those things that you hear, and have not heard them, while you have seen all of these prophecies come true.[3]

It is easier for heaven and earth to pass, than for one fragment of these words to fail.[4]

A PLACE FOR YOU

I will go and prepare a place for you.[1]

If I go and prepare a place for you, I will come again, and take you to be with me, so that where I am, there you may be also.[2]

Let not your heart be troubled: you believe in God, believe also in me. In my Father's house are many mansions: if it were not so, I would have told you. I must go away, but will come again to you. If you truly loved me, you would rejoice, because I go to the Father: for my Father is greater than I.[3]

Do not wonder what I mean when I say, A little while, and you will not see me, and not long after that, you will see me again. You will weep and be sad, but the world will rejoice. You will be sorrowful, but your sorrow will be turned to joy.[4]

A woman, when she is in childbirth, has pain and agony, but as soon as she has delivered the child she forgets the anguish, because of the joy that a child is born into the world. For a moment you may experience sorrow, but I will see you again and your heart will rejoice, and no one will be able to take your joy from you.[5]

THE PROMISE
OF THE SPIRIT

It is the spirit that has the power to give life. The works of the flesh can do nothing.[1]

If you love me, then keep my commandments. And I will pray to the Father, and He will give you another Comforter to be with you forever. He is the spirit of Truth. The world does not accept Him, because it neither sees Him, or knows Him. But you know Him; for He dwells with you, and will be in you. I will not leave you comfortless. I will come to you.[2]

It is necessary for you that I go away, for if I do not leave, the Comforter, the Holy Spirit, will not come to you. If I depart, I will send Him to you.

When He has come, He will reveal to the world what is sin, and what is righteousness and judgment. Sin, because they do not believe in me; righteousness, because I go to my Father, and you will not see me; judgment, because the prince of this world is judged.

I have many things to say to you, but you cannot understand them now. However, when the Spirit of Truth has come, He will guide you into all truth, for He will not speak of himself, but whatever He hears, that He will speak, showing you that which is to come.[3]

He will praise me and glorify me, by revealing my glory to you. All the Father's glory is mine as well. This is why I am able to make this promise to you: the Spirit will reveal my glory (and heaven's glory) to you.[4]

If a child asks bread of you, would you offer a stone? If your child asked for fish to eat, would you offer a snake? Would you give a scorpion to the little one who asked for an egg? If you then, being evil, know how to provide for your children; how much more will your heavenly Father give the Holy Spirit to those who ask Him?[6]

When the Comforter, the Spirit of Truth, whom I will send to you from the Father, has come, He will testify of me. He will teach you all things, and will remind you of all that I have told you.[7]

Receive the Holy Spirit![8]

AN INVITATION TO LIFE

Everyone who believes in the Son, will have life everlasting.[1]

A wealthy man planned a great banquet, and invited many guests. When the preparations were completed, he sent his servant to those who had been invited, announcing, "Come for all things are now ready."

But they all began to make excuses. The first replied, "I have just purchased a piece of land, and I must go and see it. Please have me excused."

The next said, "I have just purchased a herd of cattle, and I must go and examine them. Please have me excused."

Another answered, "I have just been married, and cannot attend."

Finally the servant returned and told his master what had happened. At this, the wealthy man became angry and said to his servant, "Go quickly into the streets of the city, and gather the poor, the crippled, the ill and the blind."

The servant did as his employer asked, and then returned saying, "Sir, I have done as you commanded, and still there is room at the table."

"Go then," the rich man replied, "out along the highways and among the fields, and urge those that you meet to come in, that my table may be filled. For I say to you, none of those that were originally invited will taste of the banquet that I prepared for them."[2]

Whoever hears my word and believes in Him who has sent me will have eternal life and will not be condemned; but will pass from death to life. Do not be amazed at this, for a time is coming when the dead will hear the voice of the Son of God and those who hear His voice will live. In the grave the dead will hear His voice and be raised up; those that have done good will be raised to new life, and those who have lived in sin will be raised to condemnation.[3]

As the Father has the power to give life; so the Son has the gift of life; and has been given the authority to execute judgment, because he is the Messiah, the Son of man.[4]

I can of my own self do nothing; as I hear, I judge; and my judgment is just; because I seek not my own will, but the will of the Father who has sent me.[5]

This is the way to eternal life: knowing the only true God and Jesus Christ, the one sent down to earth! For God so loved the world that He gave His only son to die, that whoever believes in him will not perish, but be saved.[6]

THE END TIMES

Truly I say unto you, this generation will not pass, until all these things are fulfilled.[1]

There was a landowner who planted a vineyard, and on the grounds he built a winepress. Then he put a tall fence around the property, and erected a watchtower. Then he rented it to vinekeepers, and voyaged to a distant country. When the time of the harvest approached, the landowner sent his servants to the vinekeepers to collect his share of the profits. But they ambushed his servants, beat one, killed another, and drove the third off with stones.

A second time the landowner sent servants to collect his share, and though he sent a larger group than the first, they met with a similar fate.

Finally the landowner sent his only son, thinking, "At least they will respect my own son."

Yet when the vinekeepers saw the son approaching, they plotted among themselves. "This is the heir. If we kill him, his inheritance will be ours."

So they took him, and threw him out of the vineyard, and killed him. I ask you, when the landowner of this vineyard finally returns, what will become of the vinekeepers?[2]

Jerusalem, Jerusalem, you who killed the prophets, and stoned those who were sent to you, how often would I have gathered you, as a hen gathers her chickens under her wings, and yet you would have none of it. Behold, your house is left desolate, and you will not see me until the time comes when all will say, "Blessed is he who comes in the name of the Lord."[3]

If you have only known, in this your day, the eternal peace that was within your reach! But now it is hidden from your eyes.[4]

The powers of the heavens are shaken, and people's hearts will fail them for fear, anticipating the things that are coming on the earth.[5]

Let those that dwell in the cities flee to the mountains. Let no one on the housetops come down to take anything out of the house: neither let those working in the field return for their clothes. Woe to women bearing children in those days. Pray that your flight will not be in winter, or on the Sabbath: for there will be great distresses, unequaled since the beginning of the world, or ever will be again. Except those days be shortened, no one would survive: and yet these days will be shortened for the sake of God's chosen people.[6]

For the day will come, when your enemies will dig a trench around your walls, and surround you. They will tear you down to the ground, and your children with you, and will not leave one stone upon another; all because you failed to recognize the appointed time of your visitation.[7]

Do you see all these things? (referring to the temple buildings) Truly I say to you, not one stone will be left standing. Jerusalem will be trampled under foot by the Gentiles, until the times of the Gentiles be completed.[8]

When you hear of wars and the turmoil of destruction, be not terrified: for these things must first come to pass; the end is not yet. Nation will rise against nation, and kingdom against kingdom. Fearful sights and great signs will appear in the heavens.]

There will be signs in the sun, and in the moon, and in the stars. On the earth will be great distress among the nations, and perplexity, roaring like the sea's mighty waves. There will be increasing famines, and plagues, and earthquakes. All these are the beginning of sorrows. Because sin will abound, the love of many will turn cold.[10]

You will be betrayed, and condemned to die, and be hated by all nations for my name's sake. But remain watching, and pray always that you may be counted worthy to escape these things that are coming to pass, and to stand, one day, before the Messiah, the Son of man.[11]

Learn what the fig tree can teach you. When its branches grow full of sap and produce new leaves, you know that summer is near.

No man knows the day, or the hour, not even the angels in heaven, but only my Father. Yet, when you see all these events begin to come to pass, you will know that my return draws near.[12]

THE RETURN

Watch therefore, for you know not the hour when your Lord will come.[1]

Beware that no man deceive you, for in the end times, many will come using my name, saying, "I am Christ," and they will deceive many. False prophets will arise, and they too will lead many into believing their lies.[2]

So, don't believe them when they tell you, "Here is Christ, or there." For there will arise many false Christs, and false prophets, exhibiting strange signs and wonders. Even the just will be deceived.

If they say, "Behold, he is in the desert," don't rush out looking for me. Or, if they say, "He is in a secret location that I alone know," don't believe them. For as the lightning comes out of the east, and shines even to the west, so will be the coming of the Son of man.[3]

At the end time, the sign of the Son of man will appear in the heavens causing the nations of the earth to mourn, for they will see the Messiah, the Son of man, coming in the clouds of heaven with power and great glory; and they will see the Son of man sitting on the right hand of the living God, returning on the clouds of heaven. And He will send His angels with a great sound of a trumpet, and they will gather together His chosen ones from the four winds, from the farthest ends of the heavens and earth.[4]

For the Messiah will come in the glory of His Father and the angels, rewarding everyone according to their works.[5]

As it was in the days of Noah, so will it be at the time of the coming of the Son of man: In the days that preceded the great flood, they were eating and drinking, marrying and giving in marriage, and carelessly celebrating, until the day Noah entered into the ark. They ignored the warnings of the approaching flood.[6]

So it was in the days of Lot. They ate and drank, bought and sold, planted and built. But the day when Lot left Sodom, it rained fire and brimstone from heaven, and destroyed them all. So it will be on the day that the Son of man is revealed.[7]

Don't let your heart be overwhelmed by the pursuit of earthly pleasure, dissipation, or the anxieties of life. Don't allow my return to find you unprepared, for like a snare it will suddenly come upon all who dwell on the earth.[8]

Two will be in the field. One will be taken and the other left behind. Two women will be grinding at the mill. One will be taken and the other left.

Watch therefore: for you know not in which hour your Lord will return. But do know this, that if those in the house had known the hour that the thief planned to break in, they would have stayed up and waited, and would not have let their house be entered.

Therefore be ready, for in the hour that you least expect it, the Son of man will come.[9]

Consider the story of ten bridesmaids, who took their lamps and went out to meet the bridegroom (illuminating the way for the bridegroom's arrival).

Among them were five wise, and five foolish. Those that were foolish took their lamps, but no extra fuel, while the wise took along extra fuel for their lamps. When the bridegroom's coming was delayed, they fell asleep. Then, at midnight, there was a sudden cry, "Behold, the bridegroom comes. The time has come to meet him."

The ten bridesmaids rose quickly, and began preparing their lamps. Then the foolish said to the wise, "Give us some of your extra fuel; for our lamps have all burned out."

"We cannot," the wise replied, "for there isn't enough fuel for both of us. Go quickly to those that sell fuel, and buy extra for yourselves."

But while they were off buying fuel the bridegroom came, and those who were ready went with him to the marriage celebration, and the door was shut.

Afterward the other bridesmaids returned, and began calling, "Lord, Lord, let us in."

But he answered and said, "Truly I say to you, I don't know who you are."[10]

Blessed are those servants, whom the Lord, when he comes, will find anticipating and looking for his arrival, even if he should come in the middle of the night, or at dawn.[11]

Truly I say, that he will don his banquet clothes, and invite such servants to sit down with him at dinner; rising himself from the table to serve them as honored guests![12]

So, be alert and watchful, for you don't know the day or the hour when the Son of man will return.[13]

Be prepared, and keep your lights burning brightly, like those servants who wait at the door, listening for the knock of the Lord; found ready and full of anticipation when he returns.[14]

ALWAYS

This gospel will be preached in all the world for a witness to all nations; and then will the end come.[1]

As my Father has sent me, even so send I you.[2]

Go therefore, and teach all nations, baptizing them in the name of the Father, and the Son, and the Holy Spirit. Go into all the world and proclaim this gospel to all creatures. They that believe and are baptized will be saved; but those that believe not will be lost.[3]

Wait for the promise of the Father, which you have heard from me, for John the Baptist baptized his followers with water, but you will be baptized with the Holy Spirit.[4]

You will receive power when the Holy Spirit has come upon you, and you will be my witnesses both in Jerusalem and Judea and Samaria and to the uttermost parts of the world.[5]

Teach them to follow all things, those things that I have commanded you, and remember . . .

I am with you always, even to the end of the world.[6]

INDEX OF REFERENCES

Part One

THE CHRIST

The Light that has Lighted the World

1. John 12:46, 8:12
2. John 9:5, 3:19-21
3. John 5:33, 35-36; 10:37, 38, 9:4
4. Matthew 6:22, 23
5. John 11:9, 10
6. John 12:35; Matthew 15:14
7. Luke 8:16; Matthew 5:15
8. John 12:36
9. Matthew 5:16; Luke 8:17
10. Matthew 10:27

The Revelation

1. John 12:23
2. John 8:50
3. John 8:17, 18
4. John 5:32, 34
5. John 7:18
6. John 7:28; 6:38; 18:37
7. John 10:30; 5:43; 10:10, 9
8. Matthew 28:18; John 10:28; Matthew 16:19; Luke 10:19
9. John 14:27
10. John 8:32, 36
11. John 5:35
12. John 6:40; 9:35, 36

The Living Word

1. John 12:49, 50
2. John 14:24

3. John 5:24
4. John 5:25
5. John 5:39, 40
6. John 5:37
7. John 10:36
8. John 14:6
9. John 6:63
10. John 12:47, 48
11. Matthew 24:35

The Father

1. Matthew 22:42
2. John 7:28, 29
3. Matthew 11:27
4. John 8:29
5. John 14:19, 20
6. John 10:30; 16:28
7. John 5:19-21
8. John 8:26
9. John 3:17, 18
10. John 5:26, 27
11. John 8:28

The Good Shepherd

1. Luke 12:32
2. John 10:14, 15
3. John 10:27, 28
4. John 10:29
5. John 10:16
6. John 10:2, 3
7. John 10:4, 5
8. John 10:11, 12
9. John 10:7, 1
10. John 10:8, 9
11. John 10:10

Food for the Soul

1. Matthew 4:4 (Deuteronomy 8:3)
2. John 6:35
3. John 6:51
4. John 6:48, 63
5. John 6:50
6. John 6:27
7. John 6:49
8. John 6:32, 33
9. John 4:10, 13, 14
10. John 7:37, 38

Part Two

THE NEW KINGDOM

The Kingdom of Heaven

1. Matthew 11:12
2. Matthew 13:24-29, 37-43
3. Matthew 12:25-28
4. Matthew 12:29
5. Matthew 21:42, 43
6. Matthew 21:43
7. Matthew 7:21; Luke 13:25-27; Matthew 7:22, 23
8. Luke 8:10; Matthew 13:35; Psalm 78:1-3
9. Matthew 25:14-30
10. Matthew 20:1-16
11. Matthew 13:44
12. Matthew 13:45, 46
13. Mark 4:26-29
14. Matthew 13:31-33
15. Matthew 13:47-50
16. Luke 22:35
17. Matthew 6:34, 27
18. Matthew 6:26, 27; 10:29; 10:30, 31
19. Matthew 6:28-33

The Royal Commandment

1. Mark 12:29-30 (Deuteronomy 6:4)
2. Mark 12:31 (Leviticus 19:18)
3. Mark 12:31; John 15:12, 13; Mark 12:31
4. Matthew 5:19
5. John 15:11
6. Matthew 5:43-47
7. John 13:34, 35
8. John 14:23
9. John 16:27
10. John 15:9, 10
11. Luke 10:30-37

Part Three

THE GREAT LESSONS

The New Doctrine

1, 2. Matthew 7:24-27
3. Luke 18:10-14; 16, 17
4. John 7:17, 16
5. John 4:21-23
6. John 4:24; Luke 19:40
7. Matthew 12:11, 12; John 7:23, 24
8. John 7:16

The Problem of Religion

1, 2. Matthew 16:6
3. Mark 7:7-9
4. Matthew 7:15
5. John 8:44
6. Matthew 23:13-24
7. Matthew 23:25-28; John 5:44

8. Matthew 23:29-34
9. Matthew 15:7, 8 (Isaiah 29:13)
10. Luke 16:15
11. Matthew 8:11, 12
12. Matthew 5:20; 23:12

The Blessings

1, 2. Luke 11:28; Matthew 24:46
3. Matthew 5:3-12
4. John 20:29; Matthew 13:16; Luke 7:23
5. Matthew 25:34

The Power of Prayer

1. John 16:24
2. Luke 11:5-10
3. Luke 18:2-8
4. Matthew 6:7, 8
5. Matthew 21:13 (Isaiah 56:7)
6. Matthew 6:6; Mark 11:24
7. Matthew 6:9-13
8. John 15:7

The Power of Giving

1. Luke 6:31
2. Luke 16:19-31
3. Luke 6:34, 30
4. Mark 12:43, 44
5. Mark 10:24, 25, 27
6. Matthew 6:19-21; Luke 12:33, 34
7. Matthew 6:1, 2
8. Matthew 6:3, 4
9. Luke 6:38
10. Luke 12:16-21; Matthew 16:26

Faith that Moves Mountains

1. Matthew 9:29
2. Matthew 8:11, 12
3. Matthew 18:19, 20
4. Mark 16:17, 18
5. Mark 11:24; Matthew 17:20
6. Matthew 18:18
7. Mark 5:36; 9:23

Patience, Mercy and Forgiveness

1, 2. Luke 7:42-47
3. Matthew 18:23-35
4. Matthew 18:22
5. Matthew 5:25
6. Matthew 18:15
7. Matthew 5:38-42
8. Mark 11:25
9. Matthew 5:23, 24
10. Matthew 6:14

On a Fruitful Life

1, 2. Matthew 5:13; 7:16-20
3. Luke 13:6-9
4. John 15:8; Matthew 12:35
5. Matthew 13:3-23

Health and Healing for Body and Soul

1, 2. Matthew 9:12, 13 (Hosea 6:6)
3. Luke 13:16
4. Matthew 9:5,6; 2; 8:13; Luke 8:48
5. Luke 15:4-7
6. Luke 15:8-10

Part Four

THE CALL TO A NEW LIFE

The Call

1. John 15:16
2. Matthew 21:28-32
3. Mark 10:18, 19; Mark 10:17-22
4. Matthew 16:24, 25
5. Matthew 22:2-14
6. Mark 1:15; John 15:19
7. John 6:44, 37
8. John 1:50
9. Matthew 7:13, 14, Luke 13:24

On Being Born Again

1. John 3:7
2. John 3:3, 5
3. John 3:6, 8
4. Matthew 9:16, 17
5. John 3:10, 12
6. John 3:17, 18
7. John 11:25, 26; 40
8. John 4:3; 6:29
9. Luke 15:11-32
10. Matthew 18:3, 11, 14
11. John 3:16, 26

Disciples and Servants

1. Matthew 6:24
2. Luke 14:28-33
3. Luke 16:1-12
4. Matthew 10:16

5. Mark 10:42-44
6. Mark 10:45
7. John 13:17
8. John 8:31
9. Mark 23:2-11
10. Matthew 25:31-46
11. John 13:13-15

The Great Commission

1. John 20:21
2. Luke 9:60
3. Luke 10:2; 9:6
4. John 14:12
5. John 12:26
6. Matthew 10:7, 8
7. Luke 9:24; Matthew 12:30
8. Luke 10:5-7
9. John 13:20
10. Matthew 10:17-20
11. John 15:20, 21
12. John 15:22-24
13. John 15:25 (Psalm 35:19)
14. Luke 12:49-53; Matthew 10:21
15. John 15:18
16. Matthew 10:23, 14, 15
17. John 15:19
18. Luke 10:16; Matthew 10:22
19. Matthew 10:22
20. John 16:33
21. Mark 16:15; Luke 9:56

Christ's Prayer for His Disciples

1, 2. John 17:1-26

Part Five

THE LAST DAYS OF CHRIST ON EARTH

The Betrayal

1. Luke 22:48, 52, 53
2. Luke 18:31-33
3. John 13:33; Luke 22:15, 16, 18-20
4. Matthew 26:24; John 13:18
5. John 13:19
6. John 13:38; Mark 14:27 (Zachariah 13:7)
7. Mark 14:36
8. Mark 14:41
9. Matthew 26:52
10. Matthew 26:53
11. John 13:31

The Trial

1. John 19:11
2. John 18:21, 20, 23
3. John 18:36, 37

The Cross

1. John 12:31, 32
2. John 10:17, 18
3. Luke 23:34
4. Luke 23:43
5. John 19:26
6. John 19:27
7. Matthew 27:46
8. John 19:28
9. John 19:30
10. Luke 23:46

Following the Resurrection

1. John 20:27
2. John 8:14, 23
3. John 3:13
4. John 20:17
5. Luke 24:38; 24:36
6. Luke 24:39
7. John 20:29
8. John 14:19

Part Six

THE PROMISE

This Generation

1. Mark 8:38
2. Matthew 12:39-42
3. Matthew 11:18
4. Matthew 12:34
5. Matthew 16:2, 3
6. Matthew 11:28-30
7. Matthew 19:28

All Things

1. Luke 24:25, 26
2. Luke 24:44, 46, 47
3. Luke 10:24; 24:48
4. Luke 16:17

A Place for You

1. John 14:1, 2
2. John 14:3
3. John 14:28
4. John 16:19, 20
5. John 16:21, 22

The Promise of the Spirit

1. John 6:63
2. John 14:15-18
3. John 16:7-13
4. John 16:14, 15
5. Luke 11:11-13
6. John 15:26; 14:26
7. John 20:22

An Invitation to Life

1. John 3:16
2. Luke 14:16-24
3. John 5:24, 25, 28, 29
4. John 5:26, 27
5. John 5:30
6. John 17:3; 3:16

The End Times

1. Matthew 24:34
2. Matthew 21:33-40
3. Luke 13:34, 35
4. Luke 19:42
5. Luke 21:26
6. Matthew 24:16-22
7. Luke 19:43, 44

8. Matthew 24:2; Luke 21:24
9. Luke 21:9-11
10. Luke 21:25; Matthew 24:7, 8, 12
11. Matthew 24:9; Luke 21:36
12. Matthew 24:32, 34, 36

The Return

1. Matthew 24:42
2. Matthew 24:4, 5, 11
3. Matthew 24:23-27
4. Matthew 24:30, 31; 26:64
5. Matthew 16:27
6. Matthew 24:37-39
7. Luke 17:28-30
8. Luke 21:34, 35
9. Matthew 24:40-44
10. Matthew 25:1-12
11. Luke 12:37
12. Luke 12:37
13. Matthew 25:13
14. Luke 12:35, 36

Always

1. Matthew 24:14
2. Matthew 28:19, 21; John 20:21
3. Mark 16:15, 16
4. Acts 1:4, 5
5. Acts 1:8; Matthew 24:14
6. Matthew 28:20